D1523520

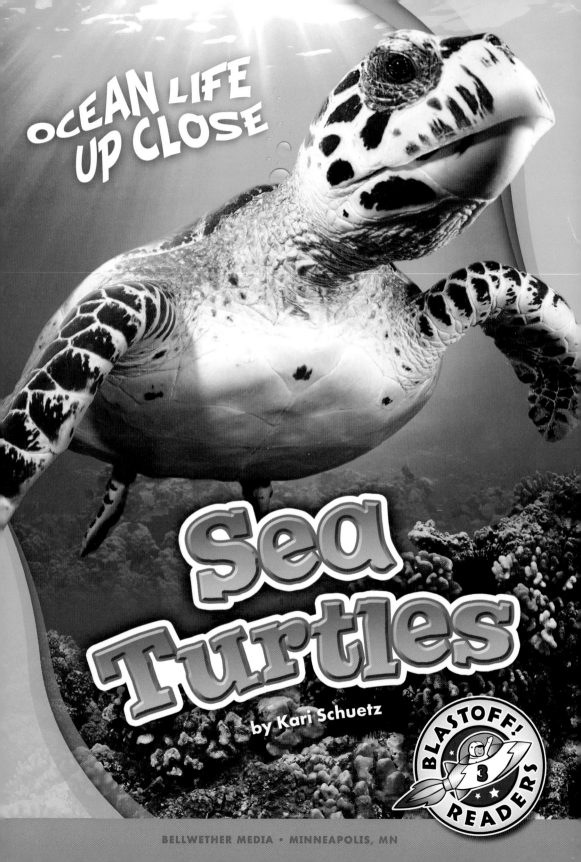

OCEAN LIFE UP CLOSE

# Sea Turtles

by Kari Schuetz

BLASTOFF!
3
READERS

BELLWETHER MEDIA • MINNEAPOLIS, MN

Note to Librarians, Teachers, and Parents:

**Blastoff! Readers** are carefully developed by literacy experts and combine standards-based content with developmentally appropriate text.

**Level 1** provides the most support through repetition of high-frequency words, light text, predictable sentence patterns, and strong visual support.

**Level 2** offers early readers a bit more challenge through varied simple sentences, increased text load, and less repetition of high-frequency words.

**Level 3** advances early-fluent readers toward fluency through increased text and concept load, less reliance on visuals, longer sentences, and more literary language.

**Level 4** builds reading stamina by providing more text per page, increased use of punctuation, greater variation in sentence patterns, and increasingly challenging vocabulary.

**Level 5** encourages children to move from "learning to read" to "reading to learn" by providing even more text, varied writing styles, and less familiar topics.

Whichever book is right for your reader, Blastoff! Readers are the perfect books to build confidence and encourage a love of reading that will last a lifetime!

This edition first published in 2017 by Bellwether Media, Inc.

Library of Congress Cataloging-in-Publication Data

Names: Schuetz, Kari, author.
Title: Sea Turtles / by Kari Schuetz.
Description: Minneapolis, MN : Bellwether Media, Inc., 2017. | Series:
   Blastoff! Readers. Ocean Life Up Close | Audience: Ages 5-8. |
   Audience: K to grade 3. | Includes bibliographical references and index.
Identifiers: LCCN 2015051071 | ISBN 9781626174221 (hardcover : alk. paper)
Subjects: LCSH: Sea turtles–Juvenile literature.
Classification: LCC QL666.C536 S3556 2017 | DDC 597.92/8-dc23
LC record available at http://lccn.loc.gov/2015051071

Printed in the United States of America, North Mankato, MN.

# Table of Contents

Sea turtles are graceful swimmers. They spend most of their lives in the ocean.

hawksbill
sea turtle

As **reptiles**, sea turtles must come to the surface for air. But they can hold their breath underwater for hours!

green
sea turtle

There are seven different types of
sea turtles. Most swim near warm
coasts. Some stay farther out in
the open ocean.

Sea turtles often have a wide home range. But some are only found around Australia.

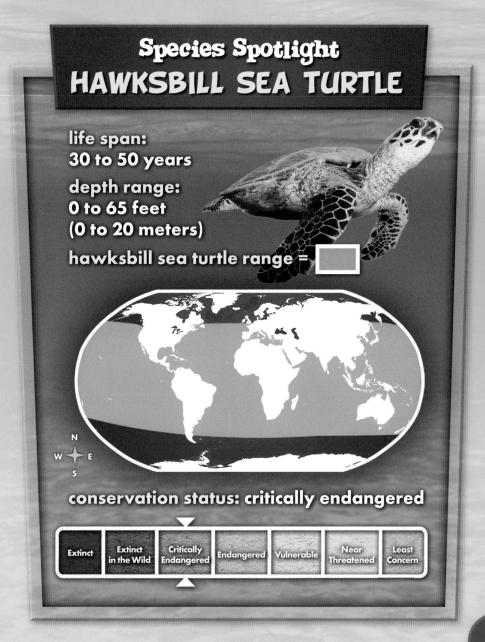

**Species Spotlight**
# HAWKSBILL SEA TURTLE

life span:
30 to 50 years

depth range:
0 to 65 feet
(0 to 20 meters)

hawksbill sea turtle range =

N
W ✦ E
S

conservation status: critically endangered

| Extinct | Extinct in the Wild | Critically Endangered | Endangered | Vulnerable | Near Threatened | Least Concern |

# Body Armor and Flippers

Sea turtles measure between 2 and 8 feet (0.6 and 2.4 meters) long. The heaviest can weigh 2,000 pounds (900 kilograms)!

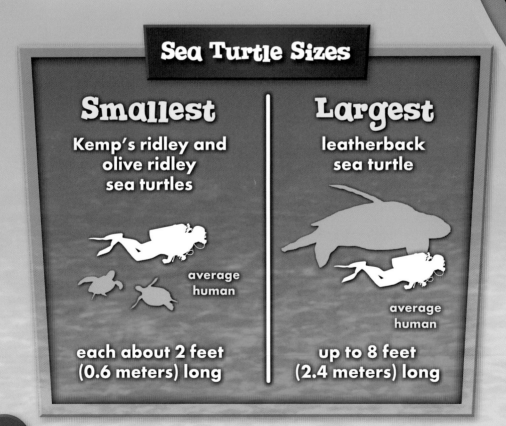

## Sea Turtle Sizes

### Smallest

Kemp's ridley and olive ridley sea turtles

average human

each about 2 feet (0.6 meters) long

### Largest

leatherback sea turtle

average human

up to 8 feet (2.4 meters) long

leatherback
sea turtle

Kemp's ridley
sea turtle

olive ridley
sea turtle

The leatherback is the largest sea turtle. The smallest are the Kemp's ridley and olive ridley sea turtles.

loggerhead
sea turtle

scutes

Most sea turtles have hard shells to protect their bodies. This **armor** has scales called **scutes**.

Only leatherback
sea turtles have soft
shells. Their shells feel
rubbery like leather.

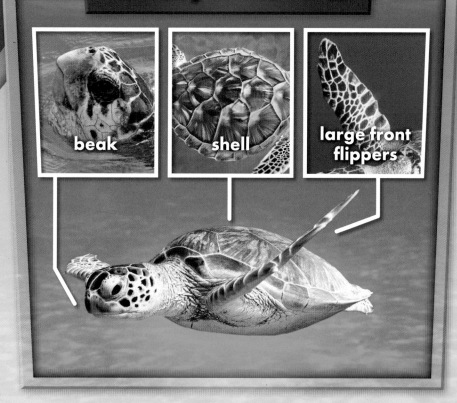

**Identify a Sea Turtle**

beak

shell

large front
flippers

Unlike land turtles, sea turtles cannot use their shells to hide. Their **flippers** and head always stick out.

flipper

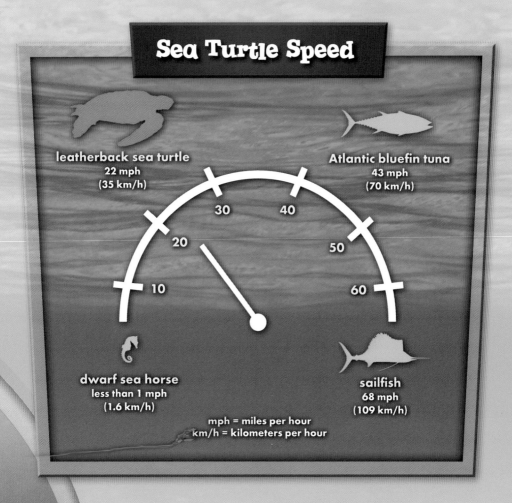

## Sea Turtle Speed

leatherback sea turtle
22 mph
(35 km/h)

Atlantic bluefin tuna
43 mph
(70 km/h)

30  40

20    50

10    60

dwarf sea horse
less than 1 mph
(1.6 km/h)

sailfish
68 mph
(109 km/h)

mph = miles per hour
km/h = kilometers per hour

The front flippers look like wings. These move the turtles forward. The back flippers help with balance and direction.

# From Eating to Nesting

The shape of a sea turtle's beak tells what it eats. Strong, sharp beaks crush animals with shells. Beaks like saws cut sea grasses.

Scissorlike beaks trap soft **prey**. Narrow beaks pull prey from tight spaces.

# Catch of the Day

turtle grass

chicken liver sponges

blue crabs

Sea turtles may **migrate** hundreds or thousands of miles to and from their feeding areas.

## Longest Leatherback Migration

7,000 miles (11,265 kilometers)

feeding area = ▭

nesting area = ▪

N
W E
S

female nesting

eggs

Females travel to the beaches where they were born. At night, they dig nests and lay eggs on shore.

# Hatchlings on Their Own

Females cover their nests with sand. This hides their eggs from **predators**.

Then the sea turtles return to the ocean. After about two months, babies use an **egg tooth** to **hatch**.

# Sea Enemies

black
vultures

great white
sharks

saltwater
crocodiles

flatback
sea turtle

hatchling

Male **hatchlings** are born together in cool nests. Females come from warmer nests.

Hatchlings dig themselves out of the sand. Then they race to the ocean for their first swim!

# Glossary

**armor**—a thick covering that protects the body

**egg tooth**—a sharp part on a hatchling's beak that helps it break out of an egg

**flippers**—flat, wide body parts that are used for swimming

**hatch**—to break out of an egg

**hatchlings**—newborn sea turtles

**migrate**—to travel from one place to another, often with the seasons; sea turtles migrate to find food or lay eggs.

**predators**—animals that hunt other animals for food

**prey**—animals that are hunted by other animals for food

**reptiles**—cold-blooded animals that have backbones and lay eggs

**scutes**—bony scales that cover the bodies of some animals

# To Learn More

**AT THE LIBRARY**
Hirsch, Rebecca E. *Leatherback Sea Turtles: Ancient Swimming Reptiles*. Minneapolis, Minn.: Lerner Publications, 2016.

Kingston, Anna. *The Life Cycle of a Sea Turtle*. New York, N.Y.: Gareth Stevens Pub., 2011.

Riggs, Kate. *Sea Turtles*. Mankato, Minn.: Creative Education, 2015.

**ON THE WEB**
Learning more about
sea turtles is as easy as 1, 2, 3.

1. Go to www.factsurfer.com.

2. Enter "sea turtles" into the search box.

3. Click the "Surf" button and you will see a list of related web sites.

With factsurfer.com, finding more information is just a click away.

# Index

The images in this book are reproduced through the courtesy of: Rainer von Brandis, front cover; Rich Carey, pp. 3, 4-5, 7; Isabelle Kuehn, pp. 6, 11 (bottom); Jason Isley -Scubazoo/ Science Faction/ Corbis, p. 9 (top); Michael Patrick O'Neill/ Alamy, p. 9 (bottom left); Richard Herrmann/ Minden Pictures/ SuperStock, p. 9 (bottom right); Natursports, p. 10 (top); Jan-Nor Photography, p. 10 (bottom); MihaiDancaescu, p. 11 (top left); Sukpaiboonwat, p. 11 (top center); Amanda Nicholls, p. 11 (top right); Luis Javier Sandoval Alvarado/ SuperStock, p. 12; James St. John/ Wikipedia, p. 15 (top left); Esculapio/ Wikipedia, p. 15 (top center); iusubov nizami, p. 15 (top right); Dirscherl Reinhard/ Glow Images, p. 15 (bottom); IrinaK, p. 17 (top); Lynsey Allan, p. 17 (bottom); Larsek, p. 19 (top left); Andrea Izzotti, p. 19 (top center); Simon Says, p. 19 (top right); Doug Perrine/ Alamy, p. 19 (bottom); Kevin Schafer/ Corbis/ Glow Images, p. 20; Kjersti Joergensen, p. 21.